HILARIOUS
HOLIDAY HUMOR
JOKES
FOR
Christmas
Gareth Stevens
PUBLISHING
BY JANE R. DAVIS

Please visit our website, www.garethstevens.com. For a free color catalog of all our high-quality books, call toll free 1-800-542-2595 or fax 1-877-542-2596.

Library of Congress Cataloging-in-Publication Data
Names: Davis, Jane R., author.
Title: Jokes for Christmas / Jane R. Davis.
Description: Buffalo, New York : Gareth Stevens Publishing, 2026. | Series: Hilarious holiday humor | Includes index. | Audience: Grades 2-3
Identifiers: LCCN 2024048163 (print) | LCCN 2024048164 (ebook) | ISBN 9781482471908 (library binding) | ISBN 9781482471892 (paperback) | ISBN 9781482471915 (ebook)
Subjects: LCSH: Christmas–Juvenile humor. | LCGFT: Humor.
Classification: LCC PN6231.C36 R35 2026 (print) | LCC PN6231.C36 (ebook) | DDC 394.266302/07–dc23/eng/20241223
LC record available at https://lccn.loc.gov/2024048163
LC ebook record available at https://lccn.loc.gov/2024048164

Published in 2026 by
Gareth Stevens Publishing
2544 Clinton Street
Buffalo, NY 14224

Designer: Leslie Taylor
Editor: Kristen Rajczak Nelson

Photo credits: Cover (cartoons) Martyshova Maria/Shutterstock.com; series art (font) TortugaStudios/Shutterstock.com, (laughing emojis) Setia Abadi Art/Shutterstock.com, (shapes) Kseniia Belka/Shutterstock.com; p. 5 Prostock-studio/Shutterstock.com; p. 6 (countertop) Sklo Studio/Shutterstock.com, (broken cookie) Christin Lola/Shutterstock.com; p. 7 irina2511/Shutterstock.com; p. 8 DrShutter/Shutterstock.com; p. 9 Renata Ty/Shutterstock.com; p. 10 Jurga Jot/Shutterstock.com; p. 11 Sven Hansche/Shutterstock.com; p. 12 Impact Photography/Shutterstock.com; p. 13 emin kuliyev/Shutterstock.com; p. 14 Cara Nichole/Shutterstock; p. 15 ZikG/Shutterstock.com, (inset) DatBot (talk | contribs)/commons.wikimedia.org_File:The Elf on the Shelf (book).jpg; p. 16 Pixel-Shot/Shutterstock.com; p. 17 Ron Adar/Shutterstock.com, (inset) Jaroslav Čermák/commons.wikimedia.org_File:Jaroslav Čermák (1831 - 1878) - Sv. Mikuláš.jpg; p. 18 ArtMediaWorx/Shutterstock.com; p. 19 Victorian Traditions/Shutterstock.com, (inset upper) Rawpixel.com/Shutterstock.com, (inset lower) Rawpixel.com/Shutterstock.com; p. 20 Pixel-Shot/Shutterstock.com; p. 29 LightField Studios/Shutterstock.com.

Printed in the United States of America

CPSIA compliance information: Batch #CSGS26: For further information contact Gareth Stevens at 1-800-542-2595.

CONTENTS

BOLDFACE WORDS APPEAR IN THE GLOSSARY.

Finally, It's Christmas!

For many children around the world, Christmas is the most wonderful day of the year! They may give and get presents, visit their families, and eat Christmas cookies. It is a **religious** holiday for **Christians**. They **celebrate** the birth of Jesus.

Over the centuries, Christmas has been celebrated in many different ways. Today, people often go to a church service. Many put a **decorated** evergreen tree in their home. They may send cards. There are so many ways to enjoy Christmas!

Putting up Christmas trees in homes dates back to 16th century Germany! People would put fruit and nuts on the branches.

LET'S CELEBRATE!

Many people celebrate Christmas on December 25. However, some faiths, including Greek Orthodox Christians, celebrate Christmas on January 7.

FUNNY COOKIES

When gingerbread men go to bed, where do they sleep?

On cookie sheets.

How does a gingerbread man walk when he breaks his legs?

A candy cane.

What did the doctor say to the gingerbread man with a hurt knee?

"Have you tried icing it?"

Gingerbread cookies shaped like people have been made for hundreds of years.

LET'S CELEBRATE!

Queen Elizabeth I of England made gingerbread cookies in the shape of people to represent, or stand for, those visiting her court!

SNOW MUCH FUN!

Snowmen are often used as part of Christmas and winter decorations.

Why can't you trust a snowman?
They're always up to snow good.
What are old snowmen called?
Water.

LET'S CELEBRATE!

Snowmen are part of Christmas because most people on Earth live in the Northern **Hemisphere**. In that half of Earth, Christmas happens in the winter and it may snow. But, in the Southern Hemisphere, Christmas happens in the summertime!

It's unlikely some places in the Northern Hemisphere will ever get snow for Christmas either. These places, like Florida and the Bahamas, are close to the **equator** and are warm even in December.

O CHRISTMAS TREE

One of the most well-known—and biggest—Christmas trees in the world is in Rockefeller Center in New York City.

GOOD ELF FUN

What kind of money do elves use?
Jingle Bills.
What do elves learn in kindergarten?
The elf-a-bet.
What kind of music do elves like?
Wrap.

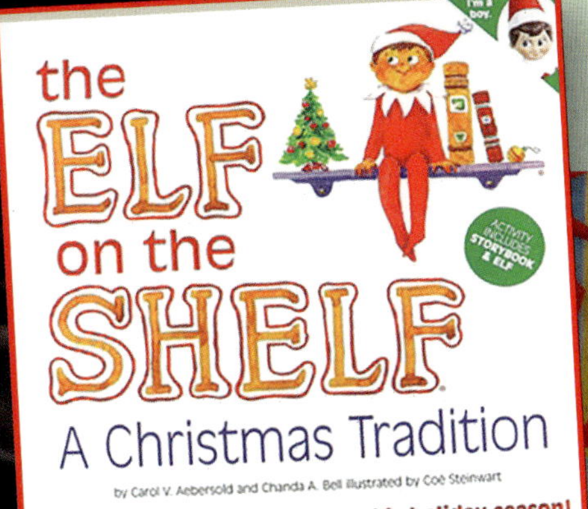

Reading *The Elf on the Shelf* has become a **tradition** for many families.

LET'S CELEBRATE!

The movie *Elf* came out in November 2003. It made more than 30 million dollars in its first weekend! Many people watch this movie around Christmas now.

HERE COMES SANTA CLAUS

Santa Claus can be seen every year at the end of the Macy's Thanksgiving Day Parade in New York City. Many people see this as the start of the Christmas season!

LET'S CELEBRATE!

Today's stories of Santa Claus can be traced back to Saint Nicholas who likely lived during the 300s. He was known for helping the poor. Many Christians celebrate Saint Nicholas Day on December 6.

What did the ocean say when Santa flew over it?
Not a word. It just waved.
SANTA'S HOUSE
NORTH POLE
ELF VILLAGE
Why can't Santa say the ordinary alphabet right?
The Christmas alphabet has noel.
What did Santa say after returning to the North Pole?
There's snow place like home.

Today's idea of what Santa looks like comes from artist Thomas Nast. He drew Santa in 1866!

LET'S CELEBRATE!

Many modern ideas of Santa Claus come from a poem first published in the 1820s: "A Visit from St. Nicholas." It's better known today as "Twas the Night Before Christmas."

HOLIDAY FUN

What falls at the North Pole but never gets hurt?
Snow!
What is red, white, and blue at Christmas?
A sad candy cane.
Knock, Knock!
Who's There?
Yah.
Yah who?
Gosh, you're so excited about Christmas!

Whether your traditions include making Christmas cookies or wearing ugly Christmas sweaters or something else, they are all great ways to celebrate Christmas!

GLOSSARY

celebrate: To honor with special activities.

Christian: A person who follows the teachings of Jesus Christ.

decorated: Having to do with making something look nice by adding extra items to it.

equator: An imaginary line around Earth that is the same distance from the North and South Poles.

GPS: Stands for Global Positioning System, a system that uses satellite signals to locate places on Earth.

hemisphere: One-half of Earth.

religious: Having to do with religion, which is belief in and way of honoring a god or gods.

tradition: A long-practiced custom.

Books

Mortimer, Helen. *A World Full of Christmas Crafts: 24 Festive Ways to Celebrate the Most Wonderful Time of the Year.* Beverly, MA: Frances Lincoln Children's Books, 2024.

Shea, Therese. *20 Fun Facts About Christmas*. Buffalo, NY: Gareth Stevens Publishing, 2025.

Websites

100+ Christmas Crafts for Kids
https://www.easypeasyandfun.com/christmas-crafts-for-kids/
Get creative for Christmas with these cool crafts.

Holidays for Kids
https://www.ducksters.com/holidays/christmas.php
Read about the history of Christmas and find links to other December holidays.

INDEX